STEEL

Written By: Reign Billings Sr.

Copyright 2021

INTRO

For you, I will

Provide, strengthen,

Give, aspire,

Ignite, and

Continue to learn

How to be

And become!!

To: Reign Jr.

I Love You, Son!!!!

<u>**Begin Again**</u>

Yesterday is past gone
So today I begin again
This is just another day
Tomorrow I'll begin again
Tomorrow may not show
So today I gotta win
If I don't make it to tomorrow
Then in life after death
I'll begin again

Here or There

Is she here

Is she there

There's so much doubt

Floating in the air

Am I playing fair

Is she aware

The pain, the strain

The things I've faced

Am I fully aware

Of the things she's embraced

Am I there

Am I here

<u>**To Be Me**</u>

I know what I know
But I had to grow
To become me
I've been in the gutta
It was a struggle t be me
I've grown, I've evolved
It's still a battle
To breathe free
I'm a man
A father now
My demons have changed me

Time Flies By

The clock is ticking
Time is flying by
Express what you hold
Let those you love, behold
That which they had yet to see
Unleash what could possibly be
The greatest moment in their lives
Speak up and speak out
Do not let time fly by

<u>**The Past**</u>

Time has past

But the pain still lasts

I remembered what we shared

I remember when we cared

Those days no longer remain

Those days are just stains

That won't wash away

That was the past

This is the present

Our split was a gift

Depression

Again it attacks

The stress and frustration

They're magnetic, they attract

The battles with depression

This isn't a confession

But I have felt the strain

Moments in darkness

Silence in the rain

Wondering what was next

Trying to escape the pain

A bout I'm fighting to win

But at the moment I'm down

It's gotten ahold of me again

Addiction

An addiction

Is being overly attentive

To this or that

When it's fashion

They call it passion

And give you pats

Addictions are real

They can destroy or kill

Loved ones and others

Be strong together

Be there for one another

Because some may not see

The addiction that they covid

<u>**"IN"**</u>

There is strength in silence

Knowledge in listening

Passion in pain

Adversity through strain

You can grow

You can evolve

You will learn

Just get up when you fall

There is unhealthiness in stress

Weakness in frustration

Fear in darkness

Loss in hesitation

Don't let life destroy you

There is evolution in meditation

SugaBear

Silent and strong

Aggressive and sweet

A creature in his own world

Until his space is breached

There's a look, a stare

He tries to play it fare

But most are unaware

Of the dangers they face

When wrongly approaching, SugaBear

An animal, a beast

Furious when time to feast

An introvert at heart

But a product of the streets

Approach with caution

Be aware of the stare

There is animalistic aggression

Deep within, SugaBear

<u>**Time & Money**</u>

Where does the money go

Where does the time flow

One we work hard for

The other just come & go

All with the slightest of ease

Then come so suddenly

We feel the breeze

And like the wind

They go, they flow with the seas

We see them in the day

They pass in the night

Wave good-bye to those ships

They're gone, out of sight

Orange & Green

Damn, this gear gleam

I'm talking this orange & green

Head to toe clean

As I stepped onto the scene

Green Canes fitted

Orange Adidas with it

Orange Hurricanes tee

Green Sebastian shorts for me

From Orlando to Miami

The 407 to the 305

Tossing up The U

With plenty of high fives

This is the fam

This how we ride

Orange & green everywhere

As far as the eye can see

If you stand with The U

This is the place to be

"Is This The End?"

I'm thinking

I'm wondering

Is this the end for us

So much time

So many moments

Has the end begin for us

The happiness

The sadness

The stress

The strain

Is what we had past gone

Is this the beginning of the pain

We've seen brighter days

We've been through darker nights

Is working it out wrong

Is parting ways right?

Is this the end

Or is there more in sight

Ascended To My Zen

The days come

The nights go

The ocean flows

The winds blow

The sharks swim

The tigers rome

I'm in this crowd

But I stand alone

This is my zen

I've ascended to my zone

I'm not lost

I've evolved

I've patiently grown

<u>**This Place I Seek**</u>

Where would this be

This place I seek

That moment in existence

That's truth to me

I've looked, I've searched

For this place, I feel

Is concealed but real

Could it be

In plain sight where it hides

Could my lack of life

Keep its visual in disguise

Where could it be

This place I seek

I listen in on the winds

To hear what the whispers speak

<u>**STEEL**</u>

My pains

Keep me sustained

Through all else, I feel

Your skin may be tough as leather

But mine is hard as steel

There's so much I have revealed

So much more remains concealed

My pains run deep

But my skin protects me

Like an armor of steel

There's so much frustration in my veins

So much strain in my eyes

My nubian skin is soft & smooth

But it's tough as steel

When those moments arise

All You Poses

What's left

May just be what's right

What you think is right

May just be what's wrong

What you think is wrong

May be just what you need

What you think you need

May just be what you want

What you want

May just be out of reach

That which is out of reach

May just be that way for a reason

That reason may just be

Because what you already have

Is all you have to poses

To achieve and succeed

<u>**R.E.I.G.N**</u>

Prepare to be <u>righteous</u>

As you grow throughout

Your own <u>evolution</u>

While <u>inspiring</u> others

In a <u>genuine</u>

And <u>nourishing</u> manner

Our Escape

Alone we stood

Hand and hand

Footprints in the sand

We danced until daybreak

This was our escape

From that which we couldn't escape

But within each other

We held faith

That the horizon

Would bring new days

<u>**Blood & Skin**</u>

Your blood tells a story

Your skin holds history

Look deeper within

The truth isn't a mystery

Your blood travels paths

Your skin navigates journeys

Study who you are

Understand without worry

Your blood, your skin

It's your future, your past, your present

Believe in who you are

Be proud of your presence

<u>**Little Bird**</u>

Breathe today

The air is pure

You're free today

Spread your wings

And fly away

Leave the nest

A new beginning awaits

The air is cool

The breeze is smooth

Venture off little bird

There's nothing here left to do

<u>**She Flies So High**</u> **Dedicated To: Lola**

From the dresser

To the bed

She flies through the air

Flowing in the wind

Her beautiful curly hair

From the chair

To the sofa

She flies so high

Her hands in the air

Like she's trying to reach the sky

The happiness on her face

Shines brighter than the sun

Her home is her playground

She's joyful when having fun

<u>**The Waiting Room**</u>

Time consumes

Moments loom

Waiting and waiting

As tensions fill the room

Your name is called

Just a couple of questions

That's all

Back to your seat

You fall

More waiting and waiting

As your life is consumed

By so much time lost

In this place filled with gloom

How can we escape

This waiting room

<u>**Lock & Key**</u>

The lock & the key

There was you

There was me

Together we were amazing

Apart time was less sweet

Friends became lovers

I just had to sweep you off your feet

I wanted to show you real

You had seen enough fake

Majik made you Majestik

A queen doesn't deserve

Rats and snakes

What's a lock without a key

What's a key without a lock

We opened so much within each other

Now the door is forever blocked

<u>**Why?**</u>

How can you

Read my poems

Yet, not hear my voice?

Why would you make

Our love set

As we watch

The sunrise?

Why?

Why such a surprise?

I asked

As my heart dies

<u>**You Were**</u>

In my life

You were

And in an instant

You were gone

Moments came & went

Then you were home

So I thought

You were in

My vision

But you were

Distant

So distant

The Storm

The winds are angry

The sea is raging

The sky is furious

Flashing its power

Rumbles like roars

Banging like bombs

What's in store?

The wind crashes through

Waves rise to reach clouds

The storm has come

As buildings come tumbling down

<u>**Vouch**</u>

I do not need
You to vouch for me
Listen to my voice
Hear me speak
My message is thunder
My words can teach
You cannot vouch for truth
The truth has its own speech
The facts can't be denied
Just cause you don't
Want to hear it
Due to your damaged pride
You cannot vouch
For the knowledge
It is what it be
Knowledge is freedom
Knowledge is release

<u>**It Is There**</u>

It's there you'll see
It's there that
Days and nights meet
It's the moments
Between now and then
Between here and there
The moments between
Yes and wow
It is there you'll see
It is there you'll greet
Those moments, those times
That separate ground from feet

<u>**Truth Is....**</u>

Truth is

I was never mad

Just disappointed

Truth is

My heart was never broken

Just disjointed

Truth is

I was never hurt

It was just a slight bruise

Truth is

My poems are for me

Never for you

Truth is

The sun may help me shine

But the moon is my muse

Truth is just that

The truth is....

I Am Fact

I am not perfect

But I am fact

My skin is heir

To every throne you seek

My blood bleeds history

In every land you speak

My fists have carved the way

For every path you rome

My soul holds history

In every sea you comb

I am the beginning

The beginning of life to be

Knowledge will reign

Knowledge is me

Poetic Samurai

I wield a pen

Like a katana blade

Page after page

My pen slices & carves

Unyielding, unscathed

Tired & weak

Near death I cannot release

My pen isn't just a weapon

It's an extension of me

Unstoppable & immortal

Together, my pen & I

Fearless & no longer man

I am the poetic samurai

<u>**Beast About To Feast**</u> Dedicated To: Reign Jr.

It's a gamer's lifestyle

Man, that boy there so wild

I bet your girlfriend says, "oh wow"

Look back & watch her pass out

The beast about to feast

Don't step up

You will get demolished

If you next up

You see here

He be here

The beast is about to eat here

He's the king & carries the crown

With no fear

Computer or console

@feastthebeastyt is strong

On his throne here

Follow 4 Follow

I'll follow you
If you will follow me
We all have information
We all have something to free
Information is within us all
So knowledge is within reach
A follow for a follow
We all have something to teach
It can be written
Or we can use freedom of speech
No matter how you take it in
Within your thoughts
Knowledge has breached

Time

Time can tell

All things

But the next time

The clock rolls around

What tale

Will the clock

Sing

<u>**Fair Game**</u>

I've been here

I've been there

Pleasures and pains

Desire and despair

What's next

Is up in the air

I've played the game fair

And the lessons were plenty

Betrayed by few

But respected by many

<u>**Next**</u>

What's best for me
Is what's next for me
What's next for you
Is what's best for you
You have to think & decide
Don't make a decision right out of the blue
What's next is next
What's best is a test
All else is a challenge
You learn from the rest

<u>**Thrived & Survived**</u>

I'm here

I am alive

I've thrived & survived

Although life tried

To rip me to pieces

To eat me alive

I still thrived

I am here

I survived

Heal

I thought she was stronger

But I soon realized

She wasn't built for this

I'm good, I'm stronger

I've healed from this

I hope she finds her way

So she can deal with this

This life she chose

The lies she's told

Hopefully she'll find her way

Before her form turns cold

Today Not Tomorrow

Start today

Tomorrow is a fantasy

You have to take a stand

You'll see

Waiting and debating

Is just you hesitating

About what could be

What should be

Today is real

Tomorrow is just a fantasy

<u>**Negatives Past**</u>

Today is the day
To put all regrets aside
You've lived
You're alive
Let past discretions ride
Do not fill yourself
With ghosts of negatives past
Let your future
Be just that, at last

<u>**Versus Speak**</u>

Short or long

The words greet themselves

Haku or poem

The versus speak themselves

What you put in

Is what you get out

What you receive

And what you conceive

Is really up to

How you read out

Just Listen

I could write

Two million poems

And still not know

What to speak to you

But if you listened to my heart

A couple thumps could say

So much more than words could do

I've wrote, I've written

But all you have to do is listen

I could put aside

The pen and pad

If to my heart

You would just listen

My Sword

I've carved & carved

My way through these spaces

Between the lines on the page

Unleashed that within

Passions, pleasures, pains, & rage

I wield my sword with precision

I can't tell where it ends

And starts with me

All that I truly know

Is that my sword

Is a part of me

Parts Of You

I will always love
Every part of you
Every part of you are
The most delicious parts
Of life & the world for me
I couldn't touch or taste
Without the deliciousness
Of your passion
And the silkiness
Of your love

<u>**Level Of Elevation**</u>

Time flies

But our love soars

Your lips placed upon me

Another level of feelings

An elevation of emotion

That I am proud

That I am honored

To be feeling

To be bound

<u>**Nourishing Essence**</u>

Is this a blast

From the past

Or a striking moment

In the present

I'm trying to enjoy

Your loving presence

But I'm already nourished

By another essence

Her scent, he touch

Has fulfilled me so much

The essence of her nourishment

Has provided such a rush

<u>**Minorities**</u>

The truth can be told

But, will it?

So many try to conceal it

Behind imaginary hopes

And falsely sold dreams

The truth plus enlightenment

Equals death, so it seems

Minorities can learn

As long as it's what the systems teaching

Minorities can worship

As long as it's what the systems preaching

Minorities can get

As long as it's what the system is giving

Minorities can live

As long as the system approves of them living

Discover The Divided

I'm not preaching

I'm just doing my best

To keep reaching to the masses

Go ahead and learn

Learn in them classes

That they giving you

But at your own pace

In your own time

Learn that which has been

Divided from you

See, you are history

They want to keep the past

A deep dark mystery

To keep you from discovering

Just how great you truly are

<u>**Outlined In The Sand**</u>

I've carved lines in the sand
But I demand
That you let me carve in stone
So that my message can be shown
To future generations
Be patient, they say
As the ocean waves wash away
What I have outlined in the sand
I carve and carve
Patient yet frequently
The waves are beating me
As my body is weakened
And as death takes over me
I realize I'll never see
That small slab of stone
That they promised me

<u>**It Speaks**</u>

It beats for you

I mean deep for you

My feet walk on the streets

To the sound

That it speaks for you

Sleep just won't do

I wake to this thumping sound

That's ready to speak to you

I feel it deep for you

My eyes have leaked for you

What else can I do?

Shh, just listen

It bleeds for you

<u>**Open To Speak**</u>

Speak to me

I know the stress be clouding

The frustrations be piling

But you have to be open to speak

In order to release

You can't let it get to be

To much to release your speech

Stress and frustration build up

The violence tend to leak

Be open to speak

There are moments we all get weak

But you are free to release

Through freedom of speech

Lives Destroyed

Blue killing black

Black killing black

We gotta face the facts

Lives can't be gotten back

I wanna free you

I wanna free me

But we gotta stop

The shooting spree

Families are losing loved ones

Lives are being destroyed

This world is filled with violence

Due to the bullets being deployed

Let's just speak to one another

Try to reason with one another

Put an end to all the violence

And start to teach one another

<u>**Just Listen**</u>

My head is in the clouds

I feel I'm floating now

So much has been written

In my own blood

That I'm more outspoken now

I use to move in silence

Now I just want to be heard

But each time I speak

My body gets weak

I feel that no one

Has head a word

What is next for me?

I'm floating

There's so much to see

I just need others to listen

Stay focused, pay attention

My knowledge has yet

To reach its peak

<u>**Live & Let Live**</u>

When I erase 'em

I don't replace 'em

I just move on from 'em

Life is full of changes

No need in living in slumber

Relax and sit back

Do the science on your next move

Live & let live

As you dance to your next groove

You can't let the past consume you

It will alter your next tune

Don't focus on what was

A better future will be up soon

<u>**I'm Thankful**</u>

There's pain in me
That will never be washed away
Due to those experiences
I'm stronger on this day
I don't want it to go away
It's all part of who I am
As long as it makes me stronger
I won't delete it away like spam
I'm thankful for all I've been through
It created a greater man
No longer will I be silent
I'm speaking out
This is my stand

<u>**My Shoes**</u>

Don't try to walk in my shoes

You will not stay alive

Since the moment of my birth

It was written for this emperor to survive

Kidney failure & dialysis

Homeless and jail

I was born to be great

Cause I've lived through hell

I always stayed strong

No matter what I went through

I wasn't one for excuses

I always kept it true

My family hate me

Just for being me

So I escaped the false

And survived the truth in my shoes

Ready

None are

Ready 2 die

Few are

Ready 2 live

Many are

Ready 2 take

Less are

Ready 2 give

Life is strange that way

The world is insane that way

So much pain is maintained that way

There's little to be gained that way

So many in pain that way

Blood stains remain that way

Life is constantly drained that way

The world cannot sustain that way

There has to be a change in that way

We have to make a change in that way

<u>Outro</u>

Stay as strong

As you possibly can

During those moments

That will make you feel

As if you have

Nothing at all left within

Stand strong

With your head

Held up high

Because you will

Without a doubt

You will make it

Through those moments

Through those times

I Love You, My Son!!!!

https://linktr.ee/Knowledge2Reign

#K2R

#knowledge2reign

#striving2motivateandinspire

#beknowledgeable